AF480552

Hex codes, or hexadecimal codes, are a way to represent colors in digital devices and web design. Each hex code refers to a very specific color. A hex color is expressed as a six-digit combination of numbers and letters, preceded by a pound sign or hashtag, defined by its mix of red, green, and blue (RGB). The first two letters or numbers refer to red, the next two refer to green, and the last two refer to blue.

The color values are defined as values between 00 and FF. Hex codes are a universal way to describe colors. This book is specifically about pastel colors.

A is for absinthe

A

#DBEEB3

a is for aquamarine

a

#7CB9E8

B is for bergonia

B

#FA6E79

b is for buff

b

#F0DC82

C is for champagne

C

#F2EDCF

c is for cotton candy

C

#FEC8D8

D is for dairy cream

#F9E4BC

d is for dew

d

#EAFFFE

E is for effortless

E

#A096A7

e is for evasive

e

#FDD8CF

F is for fairylight

F

#D5C7E8

f is for feta

f

#FOFCEA

G is for gaddafi

G

#FFDEAD

g is for geraldine

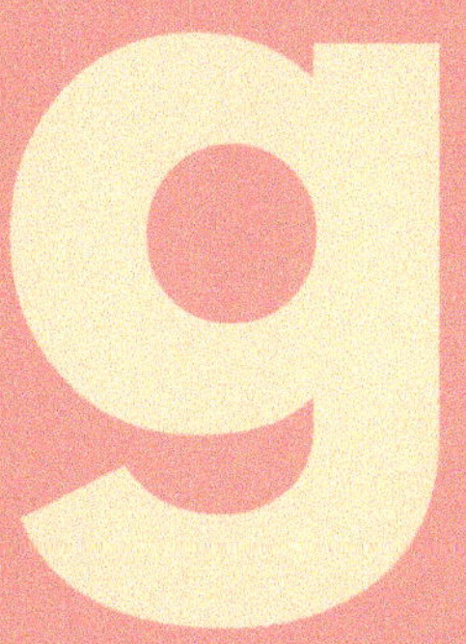

#FB8989

H is for harmonious rose

H

#F29CB7

h is for hawkes blue

h

#D4E2FC

I is for infra red

I

#FF496C

i is for ivory

#FFFFF0

J is for jasmine

J

#F8DE7E

j is for jasper salmon

#E99579

K is for key lime

K

#E8F48C

k is for kobi

k

#E79FCA

L is for lavender

L

#E9E7FB

M is for macaroni and cheese

M

#FFBD88

m is for mandy

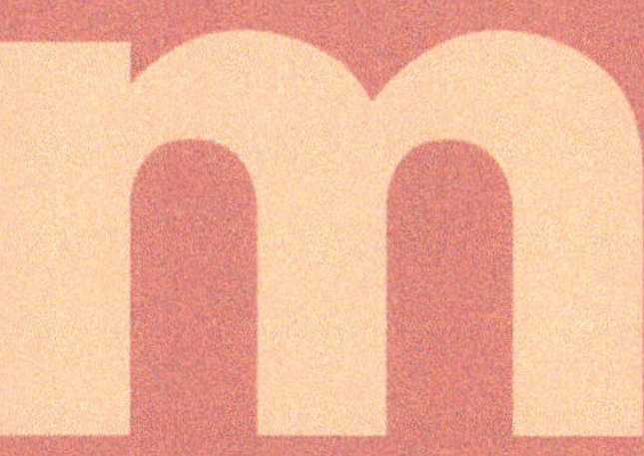

#E25465

N is for nickel

N

#727471

n is for non-photo blue

n

#A4DDED

O is for olivine

#9AB973

o is for orchid pink

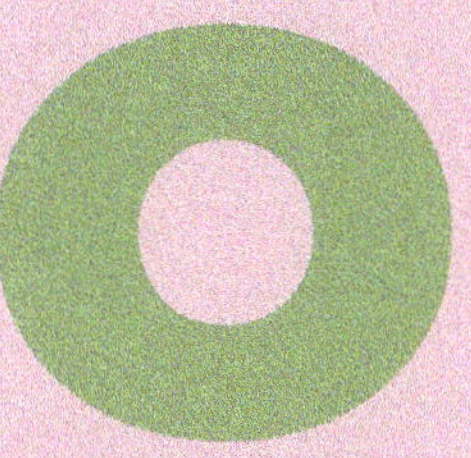

#F2BDCD

P is for papaya whip

P

#FFEFD5

p is for periwinkle

p

#CCCCFF

Q is for quince berry

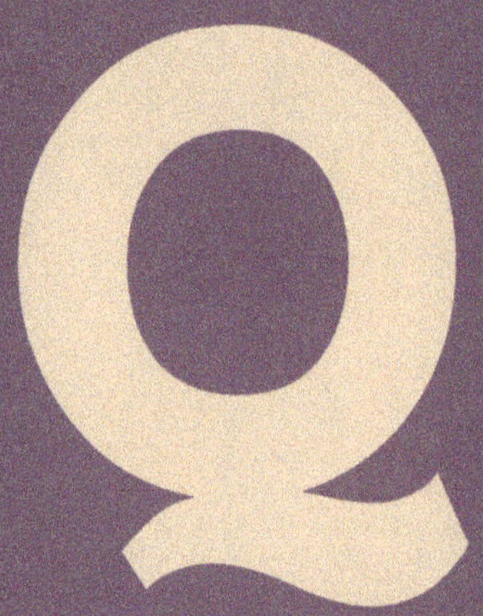

#946A89

q is for quince jelly

q

#F4CDAB

R is for red salsa

R

#FD3A4A

r is for rich gardenia

#F57F4F

S is for shandy

#FFE670

s is for soap

S

#CEC8EF

T is for tea green

T

#DDFFCC

t is for tuscany

t

#C09999

U is for ultra red

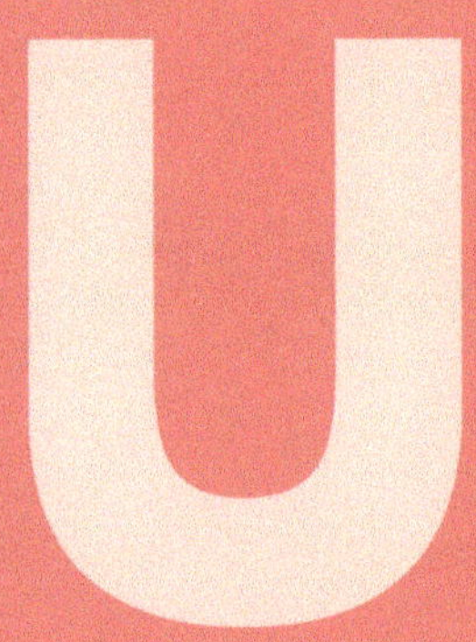

#FC6C85

u is for unbleached silk

U

#FFDDFA

V is for vanilla ice

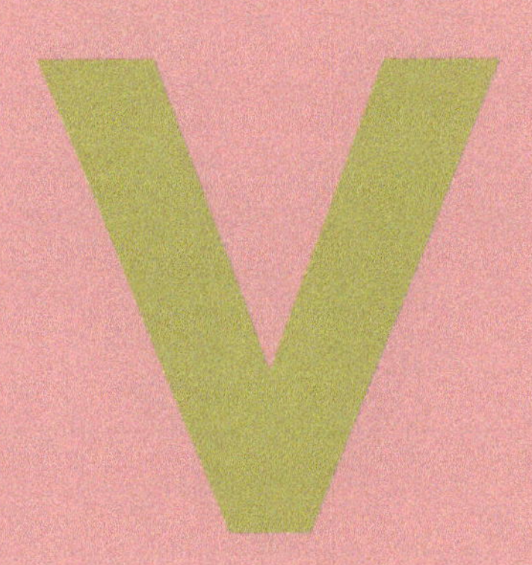

#F38FA9

v is for vegas gold

v

#C5B458

W is for wheat

W

#F5DEB3

w is for wisteria

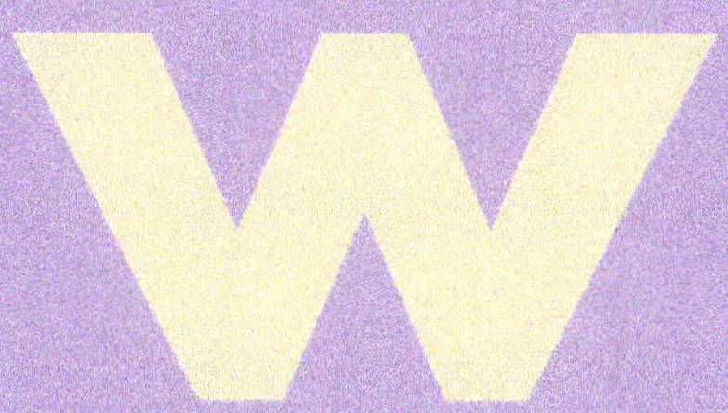

#C9A0DC

X is for x 23-2
passion flower

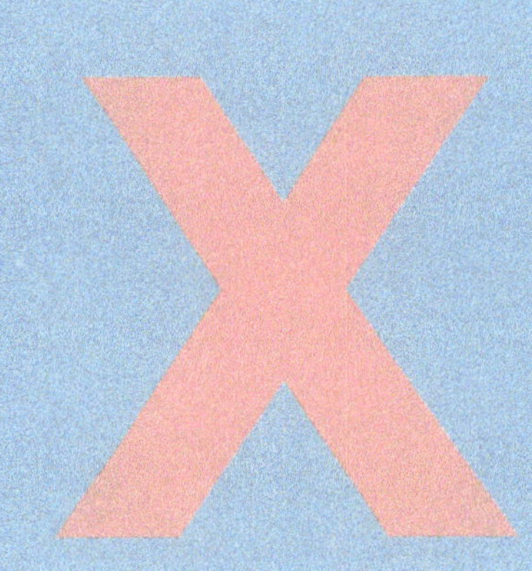

#A9C6E4

x is for xylophone

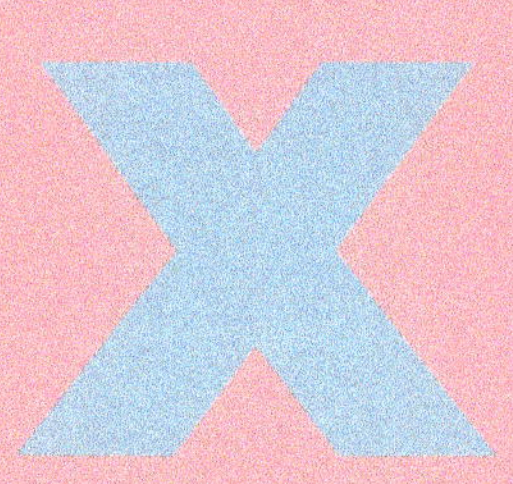

#FFB6C1

Y is for yo-yo

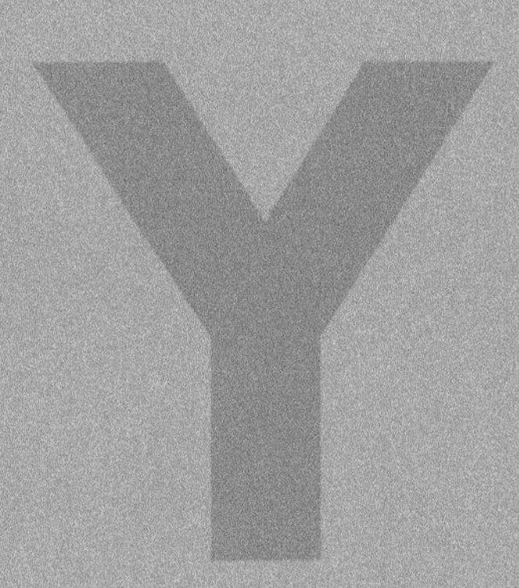

#EC8A4A

y is for yosemite campfire

y

#ED4C44

Z is for zanah

Z

#DAECD6

z is for zappo

z

#C4C0E2